This edition published by Parragon Books Ltd in 2016 and distributed by

Parragon Inc.
440 Park Avenue South, 13th Floor
New York, NY 10016
www.parragon.com

Illustrated by Christine Gore
Designed by Duck Egg Blue

ISBN 978-1-4748-5686-7

Printed in China

my baby book

PaRRagon

Bath • New York • Cologne • Melbourne • Delhi
Hong Kong • Shenzhen • Singapore

Contents

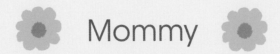

Mommy

Mommy's name . . . .

Mommy's birth date . . . .

Mommy's place of birth . . . .

Mommy's star sign . . . .

Mommy's hair color . . . .

Mommy's eye color . . . .

Mommy's job . . . .

Mommy's hobbies . . . .

. . . .

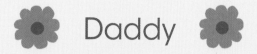 Daddy

Daddy's name . . . .

Daddy's birth date . . . .

Daddy's place of birth . . . .

Daddy's star sign . . . .

Daddy's hair color . . . .

Daddy's eye color . . . .

Daddy's job . . . .

Daddy's hobbies . . . .

. . . .

Hello, Me!

This is a picture of me in my
mommy's tummy at . . . . . . weeks.

Place photo here

The day Mommy and Daddy found out they were having me was

. . . .

Mommy felt . . . .

. . . .

Daddy felt . . . .

. . . .

The first people they told were . . . .

. . . .

. . . .

Inside Mommy's Tummy

This is Mommy when she was pregnant with me.

Place photo here

The doctor said I was due to arrive on . . . .

Mommy first heard my heartbeat on . . . .

Mommy first felt me kick on . . . .

Mommy had food cravings for . . . .

. . . .

. . . .

Mommy loved being pregnant with me because

. . . .

. . . .

. . . .

My Name Is...

. . . .

My name means . . . .

. . . .

The reason my name was chosen is . . . .

. . . .

My mommy and daddy might have called me . . . .

. . . .

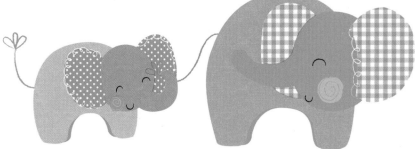

My Family

Great grandparents	Great grandparents	Great grandparents	Great grandparents
. . . .	. . . .	. . . .	. . . .
. . . .	. . . .	. . . .	. . . .

Grandad	Grandma	Grandad	Grandma
. . . .	. . . .	. . . .	. . . .

Aunts / Uncles	Mommy	Daddy	Aunts / Uncles
. . . .	. . . .	. . . .	. . . .
. . . .			. . . .
. . . .			. . . .

Brothers	Sisters
. . . .	. . . .

Me

. . . .

Meeting My Grandparents

This is . . . .

Date they were born . . . .

Things they love most about being a grandparent

. . . .

. . . .

This is . . . .

Date they were born . . . .

Things they love most about being a grandparent

. . . .

. . . .

This is . . . .

Date they were born . . . .

Things they love most about being a grandparent

. . . .

. . . .

This is . . . .

Date they were born . . . .

Things they love most about being a grandparent

. . . .

. . . .

My Big Day!

I was born on . . . .

At this time . . . .

At . . . .

I weighed . . . .

I was this long . . . .

My hair was . . . .

People at the birth . . . .

. . . .

Here is a picture of me on the day I was born.

Cute cheeks,

cute nose,

Place photo here

cute eyes,

cute toes!

My Very First Visitors

My first-ever visitors were . . . .

. . . .

Who said I looked most like Mommy? . . . .

Who said I looked most like Daddy? . . . .

Some of the nice things people said about me . . . .

. . . .

. . . .

. . . .

All About My Special Day

What Mommy was doing on the day I was born . . . .

. . . .

What Daddy was doing on the day I was born . . . .

. . . .

The weather was . . . .

The midwife who looked after Mommy was called . . . .

. . . .

People I share my birthday with . . . .

. . . .

My Tiny Footprint

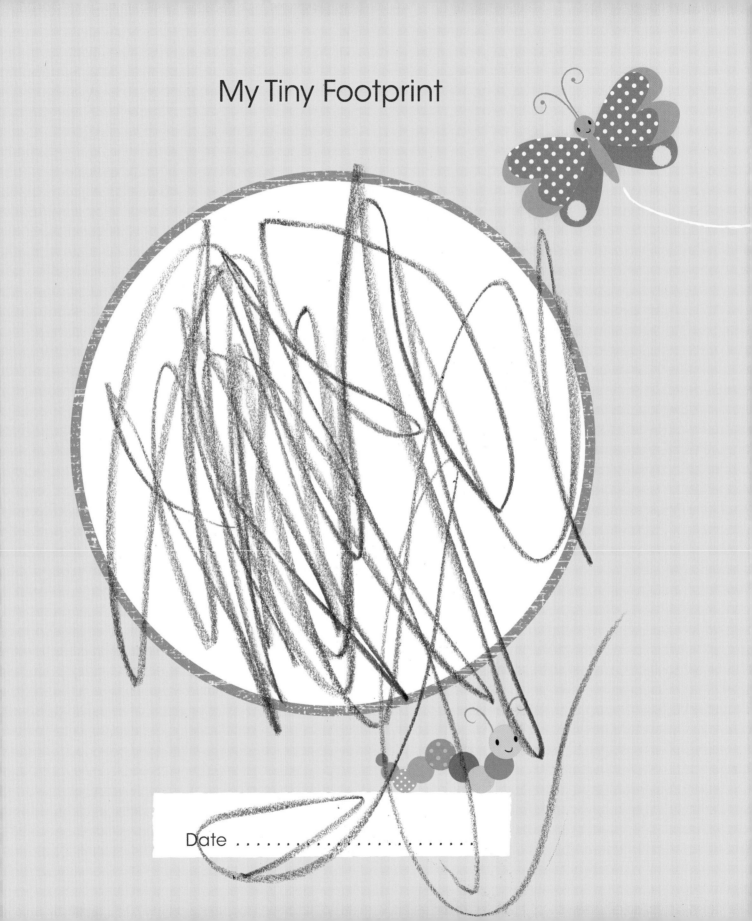

Date . . . .

22

My Little Handprint

Date . . . .

One Month Old

Things I can do now. . . . .

. . . .

. . . .

Funny things I do. . . . .

. . . .

How I've been sleeping. . . . .

. . . .

I weigh . . . .

I'm . . . . long.

My first bath!

Splish!

Splash!

Place photo here

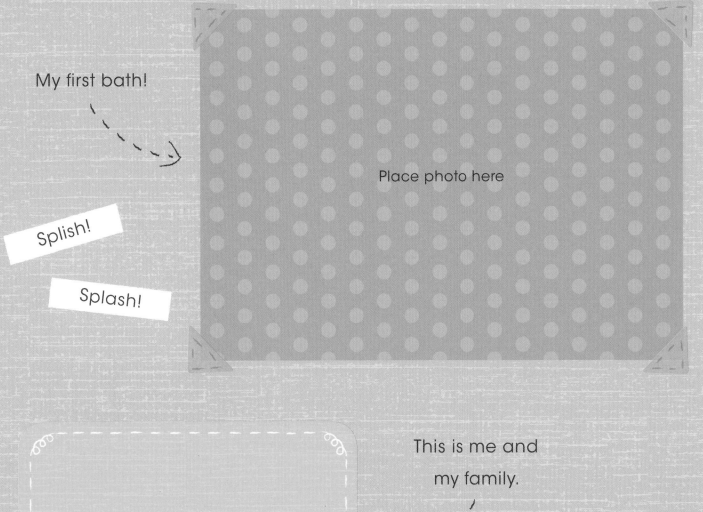

This is me and
my family.

Place photo here

 # Two Months Old

New things I can do . . . .

. . . .

Funny sounds I make . . . .

I smile when . . . .

. . . .

My favorite nursery rhymes are . . . .

. . . .

I weigh . . . .

I'm . . . . long.

I'm awake a lot more now!

Here I am at two months.

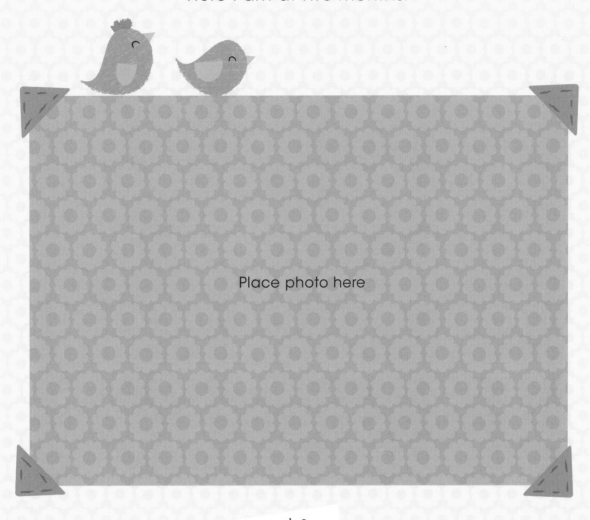

Place photo here

Tiny yawns and sleepy sighs,

nursery rhymes and lullabies.

Three Months Old

Things I can do . . . .

. . . .

I love these toys and games . . . .

. . . .

. . . .

Funny things I do . . . .

. . . .

I weigh . . . .

I'm . . . . long.

This is me at three months.

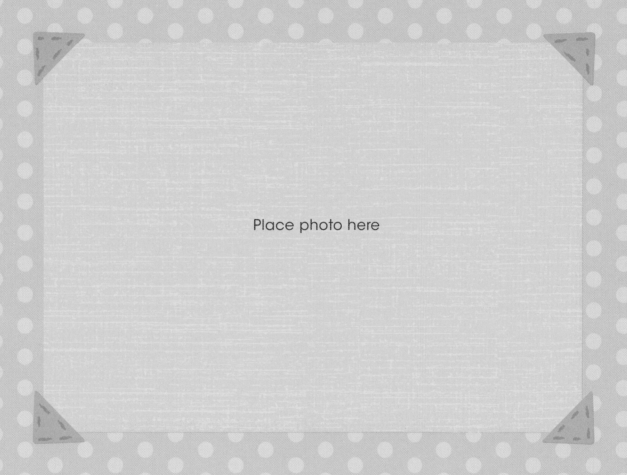

Place photo here

Growing cuter by the day!

 Four Months Old

Things I can do now . . . .

. . . .

. . . .

Baby groups I go to . . . .

. . . .

New places I've been . . . .

. . . .

I weigh . . . .

I'm . . . . long.

Place photo here

I like toys that
make loud noises!

Place photo here

This is a photo of
me sleeping.

Snug as a bug

in a rug!

Five Months Old

Things I can do at five months . . . .

. . . .

. . . .

Funny things I do . . . .

. . . .

My favorite things to pick up . . . .

. . . .

I weigh . . . .

I'm . . . . long.

Here I am at five months.

I love bouncing
up and down!

Place photo here

Let's all play...

together!

Six Months Old

New things I can do ....

....

Favorite bathtime toys ....

How I've been sleeping ....

....

My friends are ....

....

I weigh ....

I'm .... long.

I can make
lots of different
noises now!

34

I'm six months old now!

A silly smile and happy giggles!

Place photo here

Seven Months Old

New things I can do . . . .

. . . .

My favorite toys . . . .

. . . .

Places I've been to . . . .

. . . .

My friends . . . .

I weigh . . . .

I'm . . . . long.

This is me at
seven months.

Sweetness is

hereditary!

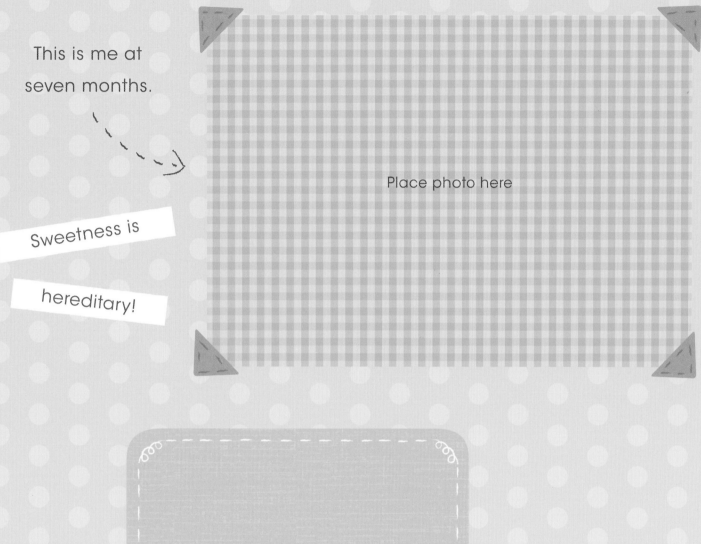

Place photo here

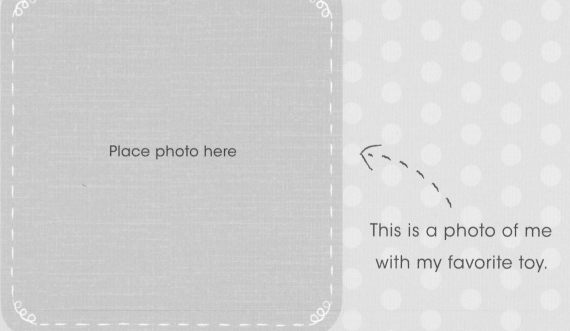

Place photo here

This is a photo of me
with my favorite toy.

Eight Months Old

New things I can do ....

....

....

My friends are ....

....

My favorite toy or book is ....

....

I weigh ....

I'm .... long.

A photo of me at eight months.

Place photo here

A warm little heart

to love!

Nine Months Old

New things I can do . . . .

. . . .

. . . .

Cute things I do . . . .

. . . .

New foods I've tried . . . .

. . . .

I weigh . . . .

I'm . . . . long.

This is me at nine months.

Place photo here

So sweet!

I can build with my blocks!

 # Ten Months Old

Things I can do at ten months ....

....

....

My favorite activity ....

Words I understand ....

....

Food I like ....

I weigh ....

I'm .... long.

This is me at ten months.

Little arms to hold on tight,

little cheeks to kiss goodnight!

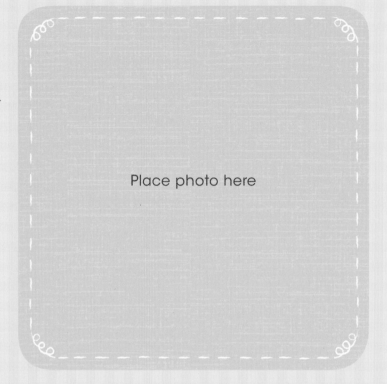

Place photo here

Place photo here

This is a photo
of me being a
messy eater!

Eleven Months Old

New things I can do . . . .

. . . .

. . . .

How I'm sleeping . . . .

. . . .

I weigh . . . .

I'm . . . . long.

I'm eleven
months old.

Place photo here

Look at me go!

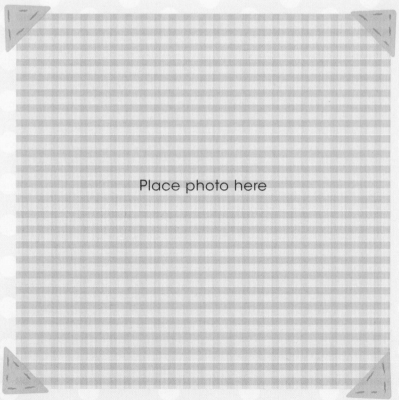

Place photo here

Here I am on
the move!

Twelve Months Old

New things I can do ....

....

Words I can say now ....

....

....

Funny things I do ....

....

I weigh ....

I'm .... long.

46

A photo of me at twelve months

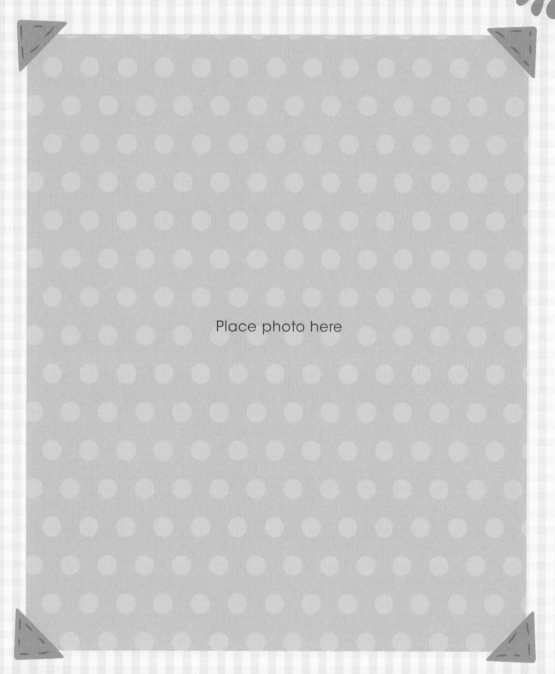

Place photo here

Little chatterbox!

My First Birthday!

Here I am celebrating my birthday.

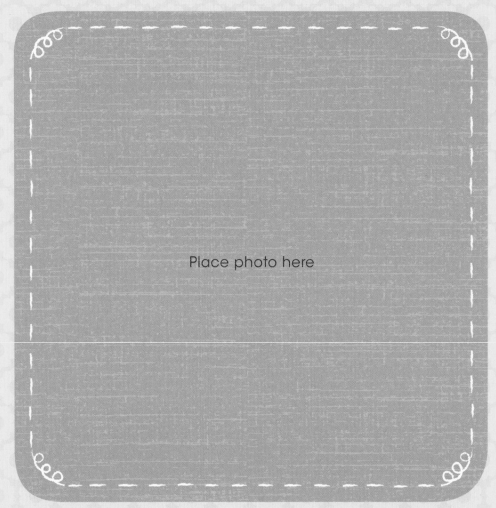

Place photo here

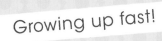

Growing up fast!

What I did . . . .

. . . .

Who came to see me . . . .

. . . .

. . . .

Gifts I received . . . .

. . . .

. . . .

Food I ate . . . .

. . . .

My First Christmas

I spent the day with . . . .

. . . .

I received these gifts . . . .

. . . .

. . . .

. . . .

The best parts of the day were . . . .

. . . .

Place photo here

Merry Christmas, everyone!

Splish, Splash!

The first time I went in the big bath . . . .

. . . .

My favorite bathtime toys . . . .

Bathtime is so
much fun!

Place photo here

Date . . . .

Talking Time

My first noises . . . .

. . . .

Things that make me laugh . . . .

. . . .

My first word . . . .

I said it when . . . .

. . . .

I first tried to sing . . . .

. . . .

On The Go

I first rolled over . . . .

I sat up all by myself . . . .

I crawled . . . .

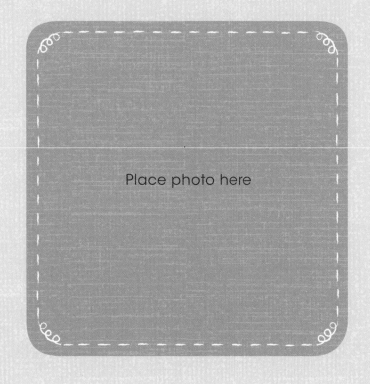

Place photo here

A photo of me
on the move

Look who's

crawling!

Date taken . . . .

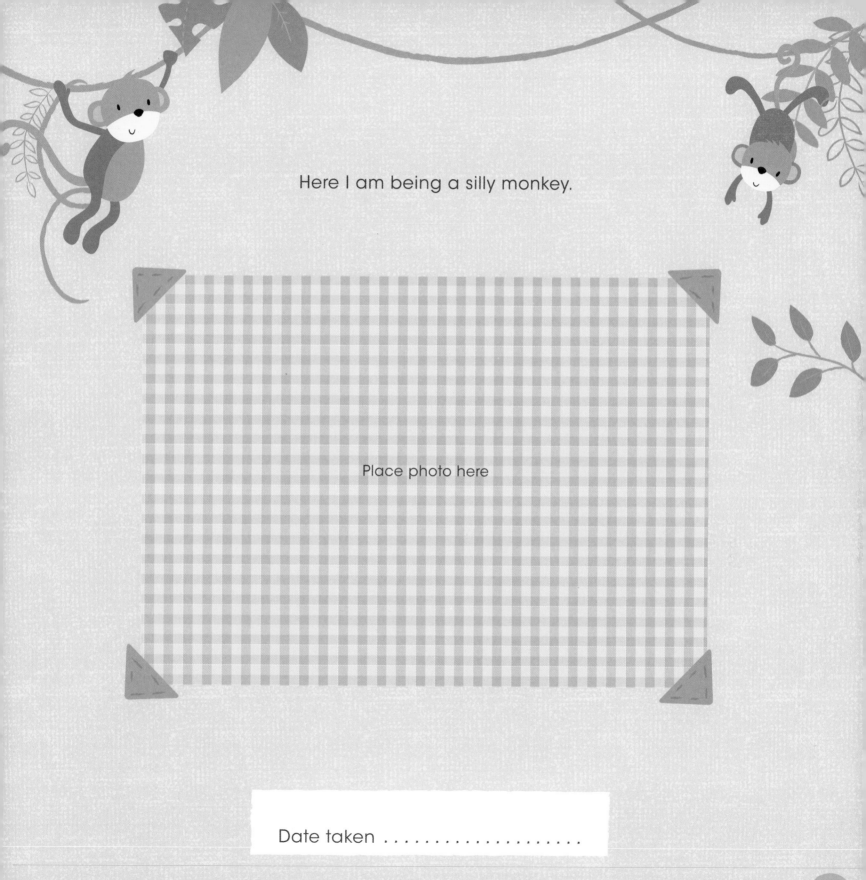

Here I am being a silly monkey.

Place photo here

Date taken . . . .

Look What I Did!

First smile . . . .

First wave . . . .

First tooth . . . .

First sentence . . . .

The first time I went swimming . . . .

My first time on a swing . . . .

My first holiday . . . .

Other important milestones

....

....

....

....

....

A Year in Pictures

Little fingers, little toes.

Cute as a
button!

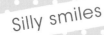
Silly smiles

Giggles and

wiggles!

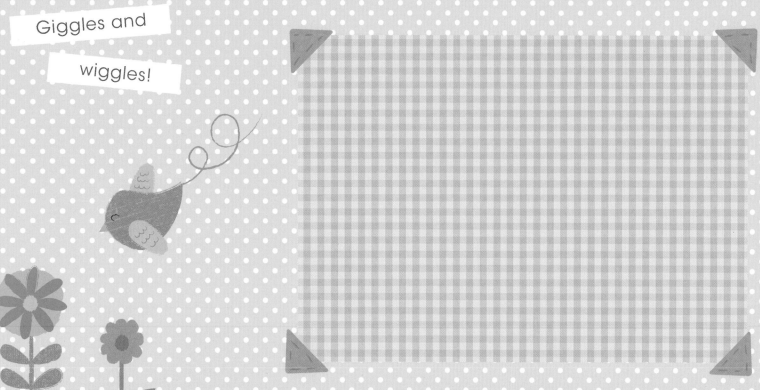